monochrome

mono

chrome

PAULA RICE JACKSON

INTRODUCTION BY JOHN F. SALADINO

THE MONACELLI PRESS

In memory of my mother

Barbara Rice Jackson Herndon

Published in the United States by The Monacelli Press,
a division of Random House, Inc., New York.

The Monacelli Press and colophon are trademarks of Random House, Inc.

ISBN 9781580932097

Library of Congress Control Number: 2008932029

Printed in China

10 9 8 7 6 5 4 3 2 1
First edition

Design by Sara E. Stemen

www.monacellipress.com

Acknowledgments

First and foremost, to Lois Brown for so graciously arranging my introduction to Gianfranco Monacelli, a man whose publishing company I have ardently admired for many years.

To Keiji Obata, who patiently labored with me to master a new pace of creativity.

To John F. Saladino for his ready willingness to contribute an introduction and for the years of benefiting from his brilliant and subtle eye.

To Charles M. Patteson, who devoted several weekends of tireless, uninterrupted, and focused attention to helping me define the concept for the book.

To Pamela Ornstein for her optimism and encouragement when closing in on the goal.

To Elizabeth White, my editor at Monacelli, the soul of discretion and elegance of discernment.

To Michele Caniato, President of Art & Commerce, whose persistence cut through the PR obfuscation to get to the real decision-makers.

And to Beverly Russell—a force for good.

And to each and every designer and photographer who took the time to respond to my 300+ queries.

Thank you all.

Contents

Seeing Color

JOHN F. SALADINO

Color often is not seen. We have to learn to experience it by understanding juxtaposition because every hue of every color is influenced or touched by another. No color can exist in isolation.

My own tutor was Josef Albers, the Bauhaus-trained painter, who developed a course for the study of color at the Yale School of Art and Architecture. His thesis was that no two people perceive color in the exactly the same way. To test this theory, everyone in the class was asked to bring in a three-by-three-inch square of the most intense shade of red they could find. We were told the square could be anything—a piece of fabric, an autumn leaf, a paint we had mixed, and so on. When all the squares were juxtaposed like a large checkerboard on the wall, it was astounding. Some reds turned fuschia, some became cinnabar, and some were the color of ripe Christmas holly berries.

In selecting color, we must consider the dimensions of the surface and the volume of the space. Color in three dimensions expands and intensifies. I learned early to step back and choose a lighter color, and I always recommend to clients that we use a much lighter hue than the one they thought they wanted. I also advise clients to buy a couple of pints of the color they think they like and paint different corners of a room before deciding. The flourescent light in the paint store has nothing to do with incandescent light in your home. Similarly, the color chosen in natural light in New York City will wash out in the brilliant light of tropical climates.

Color does not have to be graphic. I prefer elusive color and the implication of other hues. I like paint colors like grays that can read as celadon or as taupe. I like white when it has a tint of some other color so that there is a visible difference when juxtaposed to a bright, clear white. Layering color in a room is not unlike music: you go up and down the scale with the same color. Think of color in a room as three-dimensional. Imagine walking into a still life and the color envelopes you.

Ceilings and floors are frequently neglected. In the twenty-first century, ceilings are treated as step-children, becoming boring white landscapes. Rarely does one even think about the color overhead. The floor also is anonymous. Newly constructed houses often have ugly glue-colored tan wood floors. When light coming through the windows bounces off those floors, the rooms, whatever color they are, are tinted with a yellowish reflection. A room with red carpeting and white walls will look like a pink space.

In the same way that ceilings and floors are taken for granted, so are driveways, sidewalks, and even flowerpots. A dark slate gravel driveway would be passive to the flanking lawn while bright whitish concrete is a jolting juxtaposition to green grass. Gray lead or beige colored pots make beautiful monochrome companions with Dusty Miller and other gray plants. Often people do not even think how flowers look against terra cotta. For example, yellow flowers look hideous in terra cotta pots.

The color of floors and the walls and all the fabrics in a room should be a respectful juxtaposition. If you walk into a color-orchestrated room, you will know. The floor, the walls, the ceiling and all the fabrics in that room are in harmony. Like music, there will be passages and arias so that the whole is a legato, ie, the sum of the parts. Most of us choose color viscerally. That is, we don't choose a color because of a scientific theory, but rather, what pleases us. Color moves us emotionally just like music. When you walk into a room that's layered with different shades of blue, or any color, you should have a rise in blood pressure. Sometimes colors that we rarely see in decorating will shock us. Imagine a room done in various shades of magenta—a color we usually see only when worn by a cardinal. Can color be appropriate? Why do we like magenta on a cardinal's sash or in roses but not on a sofa?

Often I will paint an entrance hall, especially a small one, in a dark rich color. I do this in an attempt to make the experience of walking into the living room seem bigger and brighter. As we experience space sequentially, that is, to go from a small room to a large one, so can we experience color. A dark hall makes a living room seem bigger, especially if it's white. Similarly, a bouquet of blue flowers that ranges from black iris through electric blue Delphiniums and periwinkle Blue Russian Sage creates a monochromatic symphony, yet the few dark iris offset the medium blue of the other flowers and add a dramatic juxtapostion.

Color does not have to be static; it doesn't have to be fixed. Colors are metamorphic and change hue from morning to night and from season to season. We, as people, are also color. The color of our hair, our skin, our clothes should always be considered as they add to a room of other colors. To learn to see means to be aware! Color is not flat: it's three-dimensional, and we are enveloped in it always.

Severe Clear

MICHAEL GABELLINI AND KIMBERLY SHEPPARD

This apartment is a white box in a black building soaring into the sky with only the clouds for company. It is the New York base for a German couple who wanted crystalline purity of air, no sightlines, and a luminous quality of light for their sanctuary.

The striking horizontality of the space is perfectly accentuated and matched by the ultra-minimalist luxury of the design—pure shape, all light, brilliant, super-reductionist work.

Interior materials include hand-polished white plaster walls, flooring panels, and a dining table of honed Macedonian Sivec white marble designed especially for the room, full-height mirrors, and matte, translucent water-white glass, something of a signature material for Gabellini and Sheppard.

The space is arranged in an open helical plan with all rooms visible from any point. Living, dining, study and master suite—all one contiguous flow among the clouds. The kitchen is a space unto itself, separated by an illumined glass wall and executed in a fresh enamel white. Serving levels were cantilevered between the dining area and the kitchen to avoid breaking the horizon line inside. The bath exploits the maximum potential of Macedonian Sivec marble, which was chosen specifically for its monochromatic, pale pearlescence.

Part of the challenge of perfecting a space as disciplined as this is the secret genius of the cabinetry "behind the scenes" that holds the working operations of the room. Lighting and sound merely require hand movements to activate, but the built-ins Gabellini and Sheppard designed are feats of engineering, intended to perform the quotidian tasks of smoothing away the details of everyday living.

View from a marble bathtub to the skyline.

OVERLEAF **Texturally distinct whites animated by a program of diffused natural and gallery lighting.**

BELOW **The dining table in satin-finished stainless-steel.**

RIGHT **Full-height translucent walls separate dining from kitchen activities.**

OVERLEAF LEFT **Floating in vertical pools of white are a cantilevered gravity sink and a frameless optical mirror.**

OVERLEAF RIGHT **Bedroom entry.**

Millennium Modern

GEOFFREY BRADFIELD

Geoffrey Bradfield describes the white, ivory, platinum, and pearl grays he selected for his East Side townhouse as the perfect foil for his contemporary art collection. A distinctly monochrome palette gives the art its own full voice. The house is a classic Manhattan townhouse, built in 1869 and updated in 1912 with an Italianate facade that Bradfield has painted a crisp, clean white.

The South African designer says that he had a defining moment when, as a student traveling through Europe, he visited Le Corbusier's Villa Savoye (1929) in Poissey. He says the concept of a "machine for living," whose interior was executed in an immaculate white throughout, completely changed his understanding of what white applied to such volumes could do. He thought it the expression of utter perfection, a kind of supreme editing.

In his townhouse, whites and grays flow from room to room, harmonizing effortlessly with each other—all in service to the presentation of works by Julian Schnabel, Jeff Koons, Rachel Hovnanian, Yves Klein, Louise Nevelson, Milton Avery, and Kenneth Noland—to name just a few. To further enhance the sightlines he has chosen transparent furnishings—the collection of Lucite pieces he designed in a neoclassical spirit. Reflective surfaces abound—glass, mirrors, gleaming nickel ornament applied to lacquered white French chairs. Textures of white play an important role too. Venetian plaster walls, the deeply carved carpets, the parchment-like surfaces of some of the paintings, canvas Roman shades, the smooth marble torso by Sophia Vari—all contribute to an atmosphere in which everything to be seen is more clearly defined, is given a sharper relief. It is all intended to convey a modernist, but not a minimalist, interpretation of a mix of periods, materials, and art.

Acrylic furnishings and large mirrored panels effect a weightless luminosity in the living room. The firebox, imported from England, is the only one of its kind in New York.

Poillerat metalwork was the inspiration for the deeply carved carpet.

The ground-floor reception room opens onto a classically proportioned garden where Bradfield entertains. Twelve white Ionic columns separated by mirrored inserts line the walls.

OVERLEAF LEFT **The entry hall features a 1930s photomural of the original townhouse.**

OVERLEAF RIGHT **Library and media room textures suggest subdued, muffled quiet.**

The master suite occupies
the entire third floor.

Light Box

RAND ELLIOTT

This guest room is named "North" to honor the memory of the owner's grandfather North Losey, a pioneer photographer in the Oklahoma Territory during the late nineteenth century.

Rand Elliott was asked to design guest quarters on the second floor of a 1920s building that houses a garage below. The space is small, only about 475 square feet, but because the property is listed on the National Register and located in a residential neighborhood, the building could not be expanded. Elliott restored the facade, spraying the exterior with a gray gunite, a form of thinned concrete, that is correct both to the period and the color.

Elliott organized the interior as a simple series of spaces, vessels of light, with clearly defined functions. To evoke the experience of being inside a view camera as light comes through the lens, he used tempered, half-inch, finely sand-blasted glass as the main interior building material and strategically positioned four windows at the cardinal points to suggest the progression of shifting light and shadow through the day. Floors, walls, and ceiling melt away, and the focus of attention is always on the light. A small stand of aspen just at the edge of the property lends a hint of nature's color, sufficient to penetrate the filter of glass curtain walls of the upper floor.

The room is free of conventional decoration. Go-bos, or framing projector lights, outline Losey's photographs of Oklahoma City's historic past, paying homage to his images in a modern, understated way.

A vertical wedge of light framing a historic photograph shows a modern respect for history and place.

BELOW **A pillar placed to emphasize
the diurnal passage of the sun.**

OPPOSITE **A surprise gift from the
sun: prism spectrum.**

OVERLEAF LEFT **The shadow is an
unexpected benefit of the sun.**

OVERLEAF RIGHT **The lavatory "vessel"
marks quadrant one—North.**

Tall Oaks

JOSÉ SOLÍS BETANCOURT AND PAUL SHERRILL

Tall Oaks is a nineteenth-century farmhouse, redesigned by architect Bob Paxton and built in the vernacular style of rural Virginia. The house is home to a family of horse enthusiasts. This farmhouse actually had some formal neoclassic plaster detailing, referencing Adam-style country houses in England—a lucky find but not unusual for Virginia. But whereas in England strong colors were often selected to offset the dreary bleakness of winter skies, Solís Betancourt and Sherrill wanted a quiet, cool palette

to run throughout Tall Oaks, basically giving it over to a soft, blued-gray, contrasted with an alabaster white for trim, ceiling details, and some of the woodwork. The overall effect is calming, quite glamorous, and comfortable.

Solís Betancourt and Sherrill prefer upholstery fabrics with a good depth and texture to them—toothy linens and slubby silks, linen velvets—upholsteries that quickly build up their own patina. Each was chosen to harmonize seamlessly with the backdrop of classical blue-

gray. The furnishings themselves were selected as "modern classics," pieces by John Saladino, Holly Hunt, and Nancy Corzine. Two paintings in the living room could also have served as the guides for coloring this old house. For once, the painting "over the sofa," is the perfect choice in the perfect setting, predominantly a skyscape to lift the eye and carry it back to that serenity observed from the house—the cool shimmer of the Blue Ridge Mountains in the distance.

A grace-note of a small hall table with trompe l'oeil sculpted drapery.

The cool palette unifies a
mix of classic shapes and
expands the space visually.

Elegantly detailed white ceilings and moldings shower light over delicate grayed-blue furnishings and fabrics.

The staircase leads to a cozy sitting room on the second-floor landing.

BELOW **Three occuli admit a
continuous wash of natural light.**

OPPOSITE **Ionic columns support
the veranda entry with its views of
white horse fencing, tall oaks, and
the Blue Ridge Mountains.**

The sunroom is a glorious spot for breakfast and informal gatherings. A painted Anglo-Indian table echoes the bright white brick floor.

Raw Canvas

KELLY HARMON

White-washed, light-filled shells are a hallmark of the work of Kelly Harmon. She believes that white interiors leave room for spaciousness and possibility and that the richness of the interior is embedded within the bones of the structure. Incorporating antique artifacts into cheese-clothed, hand-glazed plastered walls radiates an old-world and authentic feel. Old pieces, if showcased within a simple, very neutral "no-color" palette, are able to speak for themselves. Harmon's "no-color" palette is far from colorless; it is a palette that allows the light to control its tone, shade, and intensity.

In this West Los Angeles ranch house, built in the early 1940s, thirty-seven pine doors from an old French abbey set the tone. Incorporating these doors with reclaimed algae-covered roof tiles from the south of France and antique iron rails from old churches, Harmon transformed a once dreary, low-ceiling darkroom and garage into a wonderfully lit barn. The rich buttery color of the wood set against the pale background creates a beautifully balanced canvas of colors. Because the colors that Harmon seeks are non-committal, they change with the light of the sun and they seem to pick up the flavor or tone of the surroundings. At its best, this approach reveals beauty that was originally present or that has been waiting to be reborn.

Softest terra cotta draperies link the bedroom interior with the patio and fountain.

Throughout the house, the undertones of natural stone are reflected in softly glazed walls, old chintz, tiled floors, the European mantel, and country painted finishes.

Skylights inserted into the pitch of the roof expand the generous space of the kitchen and bring out the textures of old wood and local stone. Rough finishes contrast with copper and marble.

BELOW **In the dining room, the warm tones of the wood beams and furniture complement the natural, local stone of the fireplace surround.**

OPPOSITE **A deep tub overlooks the garden.**

Striped slipcovers, a bare floor, and a country pine mantel create a comfortable informality in this sitting room off the garden.

Stark, pale walls are softened by graceful lines of the furniture, curvilinear patterns in the carpet, and floral upholstery fabric.

Urban Aerie

M GROUP

Quirky, irregular rooms, eccentric windows, and lowish ceilings combined to spell character to Barbara Warner Howard, daughter of famed Hollywood director Jack Warner, when she found this duplex penthouse on lower Fifth Avenue. A wrap-around terrace, affording views from every room, makes the apartment seem like a tree house overlooking the city in splendid isolation.

Interior designer Carey Maloney of M Group and master colorist Donald Kaufman orchestrated the design of the rooms. Maloney feels strongly that a monochromatic effect is achieved through the application of many,

many shades of the one color chosen, and Kaufman is famous for his ability to address specific hue to a specific surface in a particular light. For example, one shade, flat formulation for paint, is applied to the ceiling, while another finish, satin, will be used for walls and trim, while a third, lacquer or high-gloss, will be used for built-in furnishings. The eye reads them all differently, and the overall effect is harmonious and unified. With the addition of sky, clouds, sun, weather, and seasons, an infinite variety of interior visual effects will manifest themselves in an intriguing sequence. Floor coverings, textiles, and lighting sources all make a contribution as well.

A warm, gentle white is used throughout, and it flows effortlessly from the entrance through the living room to the dining area and kitchen, where it gives on to a terrace. The upholstered furniture, sofas, and two Paul Frankl chairs, as well as a pair of low chairs designed by William Haines, are also white, making the rooms feel larger and the ceilings higher. The white also serves as a dramatic backdrop for her sculpture and paintings and adds a soft glow to the special polish of woods that have been selected—a mantel by Mari Nakashima, for example. And the Oscar is for *Casablanca*.

Examples of the owner's collecting interests— a modern French painting, a Pre-Columbian figure, and an Asian chest— in the entry hall.

OVERLEAF Quirky flooring patterns and irregularly shaped and positioned windows demanded a monochrome palette to pull the entry hall together into a single visual flow of space. The Oscar is visible on the top shelf to the right of the door.

In the living room a painting by Milton Avery hangs over a mantel by Mira Nakashima; classical vases are displayed on a Chinese red lacquer armoire.

A mantelpiece vignette juxtaposes a Hand of Christ and an articulated artist's model with a French silver vase.

OPPOSITE **One of three terraces that wrap the penthouse.**

Antique Moroccan tiles cover the kitchen floor, echoing the foliage on the dining terrace, which is planted with an abundance of white Mexican wisteria.

Soft Stone

DANIEL CUEVAS AND CAROLE KATLEMAN

A pale palette of silk, linen, velvet, and corduroy fabrics—with an emphasis on texture rather than pattern—provides the thread of visual continuity through this house. The color could be described as western limestone, that infinitely sophisticated shade of pink-beige found only in southern California. Regardless of the luxuriant materials to which the color is applied, it always looks clean, comfortable, young, and effortless to live with. Here this elusive color was selected for upholstery fabrics, architecturally pure roman shades, sculpted carpeting that indicates the merest whisper of pattern, and upholstered walls, with leather for the occasional chair or ottoman/bench.

Designers Daniel Cuevas and Carole Katleman, who collaborate on projects from time to time, may have taken their cue from a magnificent seventeenth-century French tapestry whose ancient threads carried hues of rich gold and bleached ivories. Their goal was to enhance the California light but still protect the fragile aspects of the owners' art collection and develop a program of comfortable spaces for a family with young children.

The sofa seats ten with room to spare, paying homage to the magnificent tapestry.

The mantel and overmantel of western limestone balance the grandeur of the tapestry opposite. Four distinct seating areas break up the large, square room.

LEFT **Formal dining room walls are subtly striped to match the ivory carpet and chair covering.**

BELOW **Sunlight streams into a hallway leading to another wing of the large house.**

A neutral sandstone palette links the spaces in the house.

A painting of Our Lady of Guadalupe hangs in the library.

Stylish wicker chairs in a deep stone gray contrast with the clear glass-topped dining table. Seat cushions are welted with matching gray.

Something Old, Something New

NOEL JEFFREY

The building where Noel Jeffrey designed this apartment for a young family has an Edwardian past—a fin-de-siecle, old Manhattan, aristocratic address that provides great bone structure and superb views. Jeffrey is noted for his calm, elegant, tone-on-tone interiors that emphasize a cool, visual flow from room to room, top to bottom, an approach that suited the owners, who wanted an easy and comfortable way of living with materials requiring a modicum of fuss and maintenance.

Jeffrey had a great "shell" to start with—fine plaster walls, which he waxed with a subtle pearl gleam, antique mirrored paneling, gloriously high ceilings, elaborate mantels, and tall windows with panoramic views of Central Park. His idea was to create a light, breezy informality that meshes with the owners' preference for lightweight fabrics, unadorned wood, and sheer draperies.

The blanched colors—stone, ivories, creams, and parchments—have a warm undertone. The overall impression is one of softness and subtlety. That is not to suggest that the inherent grandeur of the apartment has been underplayed. In fact, Jeffrey added some classical elements—pilasters and cornice moldings—and removed a wall to open up the living room to even more light.

Café au lait paired with ivory is a classic urban color palette in which solids, prints, and interior finishes must be carefully balanced.

In the living room the subtle harmony of soft cocoa and cream shades heighten the ceilings and expand the light.

BELOW **A Japanese basket sits on a French demi-lune table in a niche beside the rococo marble mantel.**

OPPOSITE **A pair of armchairs in a pistachio green velvet add another seating area.**

Ivory-lacquered bookcases
and sheer ivory-toned draperies
extend the palette into the
library.

The elegant mantel and the interior moldings of the dining room set the tone for the understated glamour Jeffrey created. Dining chairs are by the eighteenth-century *ébéniste* Jacob.

BELOW **The master suite emphasizes the
ivory portion of the palette. The banquette
seating and a chaise tucked in the corner
add a feminine atmosphere to the room.**

OPPOSITE **The landing of the stairway
connecting the two floors features
a turn-of-the-century gilded
metalwork umbrella stand.**

A Sea Breeze

NANCY CORZINE

This living room owes its palette to Miami and its relationship to the ocean. Here the intent is an expression of aqueous lightness, subdued and elegant— a contrast to the hot colors popularly associated with the city. The cool tones are characteristic of Corzine, who is known for strengthening soft pastels by adding an ivory-gray undertone. Several of her collections are represented— textiles, furniture, and lighting including a pair of Isabella crystal chandeliers. The walls are covered with a custom-colored grasscloth,

the sisal underfoot is natural, and the curtain rods and finials were silverplated to add an understated gleam where least expected.

Corzine adopted a monochromatic approach to overcome the awkward proportions of the long, narrow space. A milky sky-blue was used judiciously throughout to emphasize the high ceilings and expand the sense of space. Double-width silk draperies made into single panels create the effect of a waterfall of sheer color. The introduction of a floral damask for

some of the upholstered pieces adds a depth of field and a freshness in a space that would otherwise feel quite cramped. Two separate seating areas break up the length, but since they are both harmonized by the same color, they look and feel companionable. Mirrors and Lucite and glass elements add a sense of transparency and expansiveness.

All in all, this living room is a very sophisticated and urban interpretation of Miami's great asset— its spectacular water views.

A grouping of crisp blue-and-white Chinese export porcelains add graphic punch to the sophisticated blue-gray palette of the living room.

Strategic touches of gold throughout the room add to the glamour: the oversize mirror frame, the chair tooling, the lamp base, and the pillow fabrics.

Matching the color of the walls with solid upholstery fabric unites the furnishings in the room; using it in a print expands the perception of space.

An ivory wing chair, an ivory lacquered bureau, and an asymmetrical ivory pillow details play up the ground of the sofa's gray-blue coloring.

Pacific Pastorale

JOHN F. SALADINO

This house is in the Pacific Northwest, an area noted for overcast skies, verdant topography, and dazzling panoramas of water. All are celebrated on this property. Saladino was both architect and interior designer. The palette is derived from the elements of the natural materials employed. Except for bronze-patinated steel columns in the vast dining space, everything in this house takes its cue from wood, stone, and undyed textiles. The combination of these elements are intentionally "greige," an understatement and sobriety that is in harmony with all views of the outdoors.

The clients preferred neutrals and a neutral palette as a setting for their extensive art collection. Pine paneling around the dining room fireplace functions as a huge minimalist painting. Anselm Kiefer paintings hang at both ends of the living room and there is a DuBuffet over the stone fireplace in the family room. Eighteenth-century French stone was installed on the floors; old planks, originally used as scaffolding, were applied to the ceilings; and "brown-coat" plaster was used on the walls. Antique furniture and Saladino-designed pieces were placed throughout, covered in bleached cotton, worn leather,

cashmere, merino-wool and slubby linen. Saladino believes that a well orchestrated monochromatic interior achieves serenity, creating an elusive atmosphere that defies a fixed time or an obvious color.

In plan, this house has an "H" shape. The central connecting arm of glass is the dining room. Tall French doors flank this central room, opening onto the garden terraces, which lead down to the great lawn, and the water. The curtain walls have the effect of turning this space into a glassed conservatory, cozy and protected in rainy weather, glorious and vibrant on sunny days.

The classic Saladino combination of elements— ancient sculpture paired with a contemporary dyptich; patinated steel columns with tapestry upholstery fabric.

Overscaled French doors give onto a garden at both ends of the central living room. Sheer roman shades filter the light, and unbleached cotton slipcovers add a sense of informality to the room's grand dimensions.

There is no indoors without an outdoors in a Saladino house. The palette always reflects a porous relationship to nature. Here it is natural stone and wood used with abundance.

Fireplaces at both ends of the family
room make the large expanses cozy.
A sense of both shelter and easy access
to the outdoors is evident in every room.

BELOW **Tucked under a part of
a balcony corridor, an intimate
inglenook fitted with two benches.**

OPPOSITE **Saladino's own design:
a high-backed sofa in creamy
mushroom velvet in the family room.**

Almost monastic in its simplicity but not in its luxury, a guest bath with a charming hearth and fire. Trim on the curtains echoes the marble border on the floor.

The central work island in the kitchen is a gathering place for the whole family. Marble, wood, copper, steel—the materials used throughout the house—are reprised.

A Choir of Color

VICENTE WOLF

Vicente Wolf's clients asked him for a soft, dusty color to make a bedroom and sitting room flow into each other seamlessly and harmoniously. What came to him was the image of a riverbed he had walked along for some distance when he had been traveling in Ethiopia. What he saw were succulent gray-greens, the subtle color of shadows, water-bred grasses and reeds, gray stones and pebbles, a sandy embankment—restful, refreshing, though very unusual color choice.

The idea of a monochrome interior appeals to Wolf because he believes nothing is monchrome at all. He describes a forest as appearing as a solid mass of color, but on examination variations within the mass reveal themselves.

He compares it to a choir. There is a single tone, but the baritone gives one timbre, the alto another, the bass another, the soprano still another—the voices combined to produce an effect one alone does not. The color "speaks" but the designer selects shades and tonalities that harmonize to create an effect that is greater than its parts. A vegetal green was ostensibly his choice, the top note, and then the textures and finishes, using the green as a guide, were selected for carpeting, upholstery, drapery fabrics, bedding and wall hue, producing a subtle cohesion.

To separate the bedroom from the sitting room, Wolf used a sheer curtain running the width of the room which, in its translucency,

somewhat alters the color of what is seen beyond it. In a one-space, dual-function room, a monochromatic approach both unifies the space and breaks down boundaries. It makes large rooms feel more intimate, and small rooms more interesting by distinguishing each feature they contain. The comparison to a riverbed is interesting because water both distorts and magnifies at the same time.

In the master bath, Wolf conjures the river's sandy embankment using nougat colors of stone in the fixtures to round out the African image. The cactus gray-green of the paint for the walls was devised on site by the designer completely from memory, visual acuity having inspired this solution.

Gauzy, weightless fabrics contribute a dreamy, serene atmosphere in the sitting room portion of the master bedroom. Translucent panels foster privacy without eliminating transparency.

BELOW **Metal finials, set out like chessmen, suggest a subtle Indian flavor**

OPPOSITE **Duchesse-satin draperies embrace the upholstered headboard— the color so subtle the luxury is supremely understated.**

In a second seating area, sisal carpeting contrasts with crushed velvet, effects enhanced by the subued lighting.

A Subtle Hint

STONEFOX

A carbon-steel sculpture and the whitewashed stone block walls surrounding this house provide a hint to the direction the interiors take. Chris Stone and David Fox of the New York design firm StoneFox chose mineral grays in all their variety for this sleek, elegant, no-fuss house. In keeping with the Texas tradition of porch living, a deep porch, equipped with a generous fireplace, serves as the main living space, and the indoor/outdoor separations have been eliminated. The effect of all the graphite gray—the grays range from the almost volcanic to pale pearl and weathered cedar-shingle gray—is cool and refreshing, similar to walking into a stone-lined cave or castle.

Yet these interiors are filled with light. A lap pool visible from a guestroom adds its sparkle and glitter, lined with pale stone and suggesting a kind of trough in harmony with the gritty elements of the design. Accents in the house also reflect natural materials—rushes, reeds, grasses. The only non-gray color StoneFox used also references nature—a pale, succulent, cactus green to upholster sofa cushions.

Why isn't the effect hard and cold? Stone says it is how the scale of the gray is used—generously, unstintingly, as if the color itself were transmuted into an interior architectural building material. The strength of the Texas sun does temper the effect, but the gray still feels strong—straight from the quarry. Fabrics, mostly in the softer pearl tones of gray, contrast with the volume of stone and stone-like materials used inside.

There is no question that a strong sense of the raw power of stone informed the selections of the interior materials as well as the layout of space within. Yet the effect is serene and calming, almost gentle.

Stainless steel sofas at right angles to each other were commissioned by Stonefox from the Danish designer David Weeks.

The deceptively simple architectural design by Lake | Flato provides a contrast to the angular sculpture by Tony Smith.

Furniture includes a Vladimir Kagan sofa and a Nakashima table; folios by Anselm Kiefer lie on a viewing stand behind a small loveseat.

The beds, the linens, and the stacked felt
ottomans are all designed by Stonefox
and reference Joseph Bueys.

OPPOSITE **Rough matte surfaces and finishes yield a depth of color and provide for a sophisticated variation of tone as light moves through the airy rooms.**

BELOW **The transparency of the house both warms and beckons at night.**

Platinum Print

ANTONY TODD

Empty, the dining room of his 1840s Greenwich Village duplex is an oasis of serenity for Australian-born Antony Todd—a necessary condition as he is one of New York's most sought-after gala and party planners. Full, the dining room is transformed into a stage from which he entertains with great energy and imagination.

Todd's personal living space provides a contrast to the pace of his professional life—the rooms flow into each other with an effortless assurance of both the control of color, and the scale and finish of pieces he has had made especially for his home. The oak pedestal dining table, for example, is finished in a deep tobacco brown that harmonizes with the black-and-ochre-veined marble mantel and a pair of neoclassic marble-and-bronze consoles placed to each side of the fireplace. A large painting entitled St. Francois by Thomas Fougeirol picks up the grays and blacks of furnishings. French doors from the entry lead into this space, and additional pairs open onto a lovely sunroom with views of a back garden.

The color of the walls of the living room is the same as the dining room, but the palette changes to incorporate chocolate, chamois, barley and mushroom tones. Upstairs the tone shifts to whites—brick walls painted white, wool panels curtaining the bed, itself upholstered in linen, natural sisal covering the floor. Considered as a sequence of movement from dark to light, the duplex uses shadow-shades leading into warm, organic neutrals veering toward the sun and then, above stairs, simplicity of white and light.

One of a pair of antique mirrored panels rests atop a 1920s bronze-and-marble console table. Platinum gray walls provide a soft, muffled coloring.

A table of Todd's design in the dining room. High-gloss ivory paint picks out the neoclassical moldings.

OPPOSITE **Corinthian pilasters flank the entry to the dining room with a view towards a small porch beyond.**

BELOW **Small drawings are boldly matted in field of white.**

Subtle mushroom grays and taupes fill the living room. Solid fabrics accentuate the sculptural shapes of the furniture.

Irish Aire

CLODAGH

The decision to take a monochromatic approach to the execution of an interior is sometimes the effect of powerful natural elements that do a perfectly fine job of speaking for themselves. The Irish-born, New York-based interior designer Clodagh has an almost atavistic receptivity to this situation, which she has expressed in the White Horse Spa on the west coast of Ireland. The elements of nature—wind, sea, stone, wood, the dazzle of glittering waves—are harnessed and put to use in as much their natural state as she can devise.

The spa has been carved out of the cellar space underneath the main lodge at Doonbeg, a new building that references great Anglo-Irish country houses of the past. Upstairs all is Windsor and Orkney chairs, roaring fires, chintz, but downstairs is composed of honed limestone, massive square-cut plunge pools and Venetian plaster walls in delicate shades of stone and sere grasses. Clodagh relished the chance to exploit the indigenous materials of an area of such consummate, rugged beauty, incorporating local stone and reclaimed local wood and working with local craftspeople to produce a tranquil and restorative ambience. Wide plank hardwood flooring,

"BuxyBlue" stone, tables, lighting fixtures all harmonize because of the intelligent application of maximizing what the land itself had to give.

Her color choice throughout—and quite possibly a reflection of her interest in the principles of feng shui—is a soothing, honey-hued copper, a mineral whose properties have long been associated with good health and well-being. The copper streaks in the natural fieldstone have been interpreted through polished walls, upholsteries and works of art. The color is also very flattering to natural skin tones.

Soft copper, nougat, and honey tones expressed in texture of stone, metal mesh, polished concrete, and wood.

Organic shapes and natural materials from local sources are used throughout the spa. The reception room features wood furniture and carpeting indigenous to County Clare.

OPPOSITE *Alder Disk* by Brent Comer of
Clodagh Collection is installed at the end
of a hallway leading to treatment rooms.

BELOW Plunge pools of natural stone
are illuminated by an overhead light
fixture of thin, sheared stone in a
metal-mesh box frame.

BELOW **Wooden objects—lamp base, low table, serving tray, sideboard— all the work of local craftspeople.**

OPPOSITE **A painting by Espen Elborg, bench by Douglas Thayer, wood jug by Tucker Robbins, all members of Clodagh Collection design team.**

Crystal Palace

PHILIPPE STARCK

In 2003 Baccarat established its international headquarters in the Hotel de Noailles, the former home of Marie-Laure de Noailles, the great Parisian collector and patron of avant-garde artists and writers of the early twentieth century. Philippe Starck was selected to transform the venerable building into a complex including a restaurant, a museum gallery, a ballroom, corporate offices and a large boutique.

Founded in 1764 during the reign of Louis XV, Baccarat was the first French cristallerie to produce chandeliers and sconces. The pure, utterly colorless expression of the art form captivated Starck. The alchemy of producing crystal—the air, earth, water, and fireness of the process—inspired him to concentrate on a world of illusion he finds in the glitter of lights sparkling off the cut facets.

The VIP lounge of the Baccarat boutique and the boutique itself are a monochrome expression of one of crystal's elements: lead (earth), which he has interpreted by transmuting here the color of lead as a kind of silver- or platinum-wash, applied to the entire interior. Not only in the boutique but in the museum gallery also, the walls are actually crude concrete, polished to provide a subtle glimmer. The table and satin upholstered chairs recede somewhat in the presence of two magnificent Baccarat chandeliers—easily the size and scale of those in the Hall of Mirrors at Versailles.

The Baccarat boutique incorporates all the elements of Starck's design: crystal, satin, polished and pigmented concrete.

For the museum gallery Starck created crystal bases for the long tables; the chairs are custom designs for Baccarat.

OVERLEAF LEFT The boutique includes a table base in Baccarat crystal that is almost forty feet long.

OVERLEAF RIGHT Vitrines in the museum gallery display the company's storied past.

OPPOSITE **"Tuzla" chandelier.**

BELOW **Aluminum chairs, bright
as mirrors, line the display tables.**

BELOW   Baccarat was the originator of jewel-colored crystal, such as the ruby tumblers.

OPPOSITE   Starck created waist-high caryatids of steel to support crystal showcases for Baccarat's jewelry collection.

OVERLEAF   Gerard Garouste painted a fantasy backdrop for the ceiling of the museum gallery referencing a crystal chess set and towering over vitrines containing some of Baccarat's most famous historic vases and centerpieces.

My White

DANIEL DE SIENA AND CHRISTOPHER JONES

"My White" is the title Carole Hyatt gives to her living room overlooking the American Museum of Natural History. The vivid green—some might call it key lime pie and others might say chartreuse—provides a powerful backdrop for a collection of Pop and Op Art whose artists would applaud the choice.

Furnishings inspired by Vladimar Kagan's designs are all covered in an extraordinary shade of Ultrasuede; a classic black leather Ward Bennett chair is reimagined in the bold green and botton-tufted velvet. The banquette under the south-facing window is also covered in Ultrasuede while pull-arm chairs, a table, and a stand made for small sculpture are lacquered the same electric green.

Daniel De Siena and Christopher Jones experimented to find the shade Carole had in mind—the mind's eye being its own color-chart. More than a dozen paint samples went on the wall before the final selection. As dominant as the color is, it doesn't overpower the collection itself. Each work maintains its stature, highlighted by a carefully calibrated lighting scheme.

The view of the park surrounding the museum—spring green with all its fresh yellow— was an inspiration. Carole Hyatt believes that bringing nature into a New York City apartment is all important. There are no draperies—the plainest white shades roll down to protect the room from glare and heat in the summer months.

Works of art displayed on a lacquered ledge: *Thanksgiving Day 1973-74*, a ceramic tile by Helen Frankenthaler, *Rear View Mirror* by Allan d'Arcangelo, a plaster study by George Segal; Tina Spiro's *View of Toledo* hangs behind them.

OVERLEAF **Vivid greens become a neutral field for the display of contemporary art and connect to the foliage of the park beyond.**

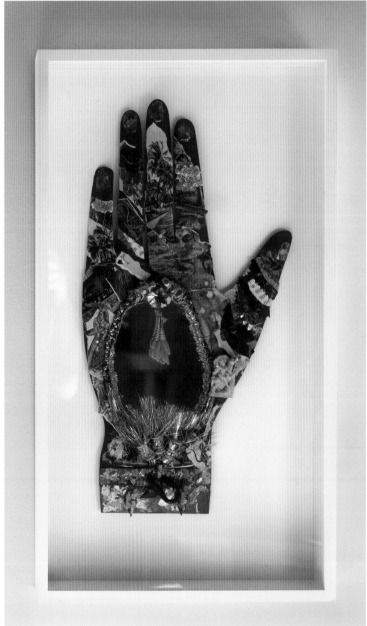

In the entry hall, a pair of chairs by Joe Columbo, *Fala* (at $^1/_3$ scale) by Neil Estern, bronze nude by Rupert Getzen, and *Spring Painting* by Joan Snyder.

The living room seating, all upholstered in Ultrasuede, accommodates two dozen guests comfortably. The cube holds crushed cans from Piel's Brewery and the glass shelves display images of women from many artists' perspectives.

The Color of Thunder

MARCEL WANDERS

The name THOR usually refers to the bearded Norse god of thunder, but in this case it is an acronym for The Hotel on Rivington, the new cultural fuel of its Lower East Side neighborhood. The twenty-one-story glass building is a surprise, set as it is in a streetscape of nineteenth-century tenements, six-stories high, brick-faced, and almost venerable by now. Hotelier Paul Stallings recognized the potential for reinvigorating this neglected area of Manhattan so THOR does allude to the Scandinavian reference as an omen of power and change.

It is unusual for the Dutch product designer Marcel Wanders to design an interior. THOR is executed in the color of thunder. Steel grays, cloudy grays, massive, soaring ceiling—all suggest a potential explosion of activity. The image of a storm pervades the space—cloud-like colors are used in a pattern-on-pattern of strong graphics expressed in a palette of tone-on-tone of gray and misty whites. On sunny days, the grays lose their somber tone and recede to an elegant backdrop for the European crowd that frequents THOR. At night, the grays provide a visual drama that enhances the restaurant's glamour. It is a decidedly masculine interior, which would suggest a purist's strict vision, but the happy mix of prints and patterns takes the seriousness out of the rooms and provides instead a light-hearted approach more in keeping with the spirit of Wanders's designs.

The notion of "burnt furniture" is a concept Wanders initiated for this project. A geometric pattern in black-and-white Bisazza tile adds texture to the lobby.

The entrance to the restaurant from the hotel lobby is sculpted styrene. Walls are covered in a metallic material designed and manufactured specially for THOR.

OVERLEAF LEFT The main dining room is roofed with glass providing dramatic views of the surrounding nineteenth-century tenements.

OVERLEAF RIGHT Black steel super-structure covers the stairway to the restrooms.

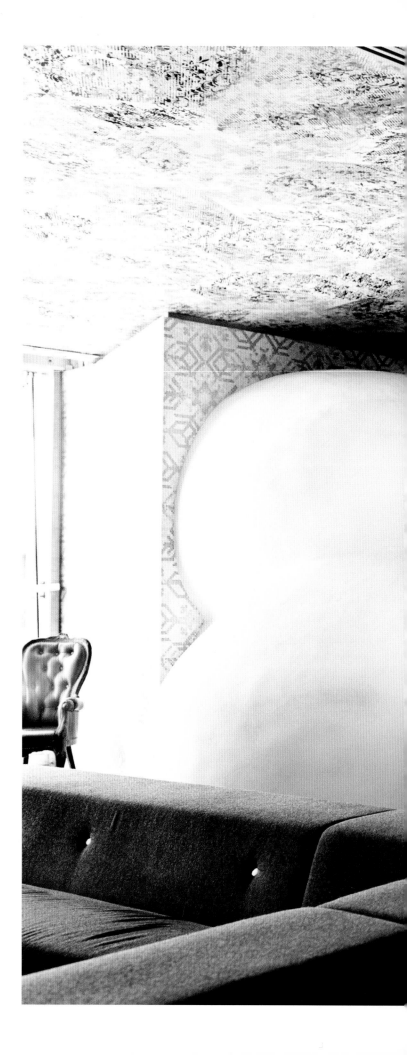

BELOW **Lavatory basins reference
Delft tiles.**

OPPOSITE **Black-and-white wallcovering
with a pronounced metallic finish has the
neutral graphic impact of a classic toile;
Wanders designed the black bar chairs.**

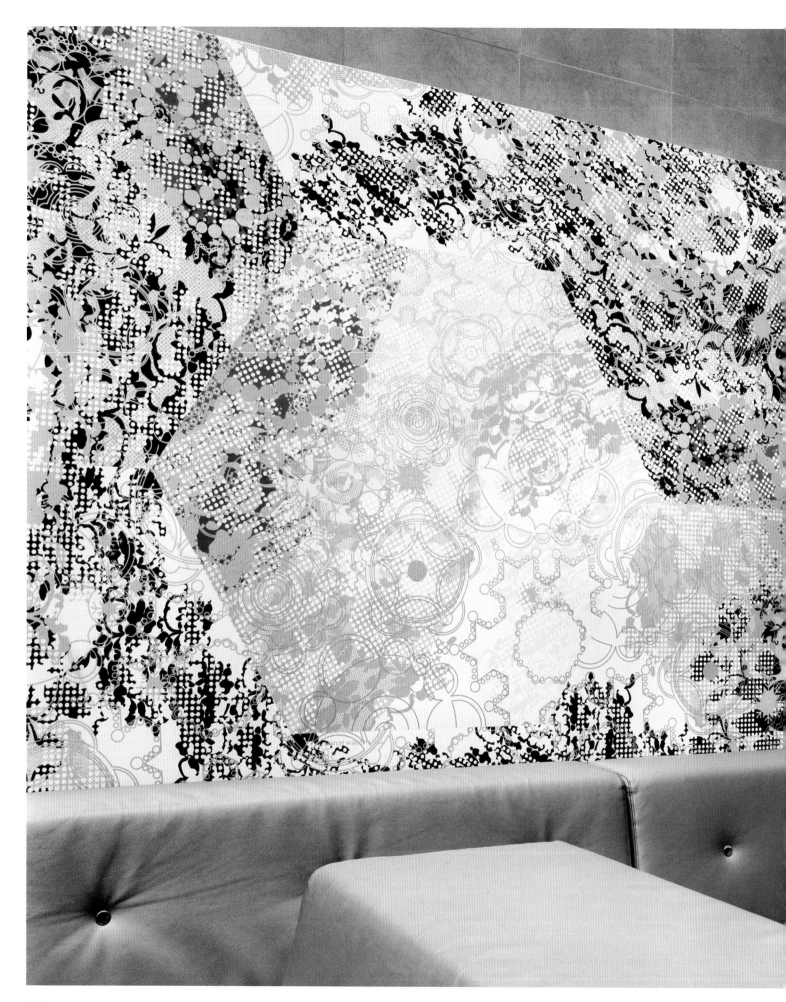

An unexpected splash of yellow—the color of optimism. Abstracted flowers read through a calculated chaos of black and white.

OVERLEAF The volume of black steel looms with a mysterious sculptural presence in THOR's dining room.

Ex Libris

ORLANDO DIAZ-AZCUY

Orlando Diaz-Azcuy was among the first contemporary interior designers to establish white—pure sun-bleached white—as a color with which to completely decorate a house or apartment. His white expressed a freedom from color that was fresh and invigorating. Nevertheless, when he decided to do a library in his San Francisco apartment, his thought was to look back, way back to the fourteenth century and its rich, saturated painting traditions. Diaz-Azcuy says he always wanted to execute a library in green—darker even than malachite—instead of the more traditional reds found in Italy and England. He intended to create an elegant, sensuous cocoon, a retreat where his experience of his day could be altered by adjusting the light.

The room is dark and intentionally so. Diaz-Azcuy used a system called Stretchwall over which he upholstered a dark green silk. To emphasize the glossy richness of the fabric, he added wall panels chamfered a portion of the way up the height of the wall to reference the neoclassical elements throughout the apartment. Door frames were marbeleized in a classical black-and-white veining, and the ceiling was conceived to resemble fourteenth-century Italian gold-ground paintings. Two chaises longues, designed by Diaz-Azcuy, provide some of the seating, and both were made long enough to sleep in, which makes this jewel-like interior a practical guest room when needed.

A gilded ceiling showers light in the jewel-box library. Archangels stand in gilded entablatured boxes on either side of the door.

BELOW **A faux-marbre painted finish dresses a door.**

OPPOSITE **A pair of gilded chairs contrast with a Chinese coromandel chest.**

Lua

RYSIA SUCHECKA / NBBJ

Lua glows with a rich, caramelized color that suggests the top of a classic Spanish flan.

Designer Rysia Suchecka, a partner in the Seattle-based firm NBBJ, says that this rich color was chosen to symbolize the radiant heat of the character and food of the Latin cultures. The color also evokes the flaming shards of light that shoot off the windows of Manhattan skyscrapers reflecting the setting sun in the west. Sited right on the banks of the Hudson, in Hoboken, New Jersey, Lua has spectacular, unobstructed views of the entire island of Manhattan.

Recognizing that what gets the party started is the central gathering point of the bar, Suchecka devised an amber-colored, poured-resin, interior-lighted, elliptically-shaped "stone" counter from which everything radiates outward and upward in ochre, honey, butterscotch, even sometimes mango-colored hues to enclose the entire 3,000 square foot space. The resin sweeps upward and is capped at the top of the walls. Small, star-like pendant lamps hang at random spots to illumine the interior. Mango-colored pillars support the lighting overhead—casting pools downward making each small dining table its own private space.

The restaurant has three tiers with the bar as the central, lower "plaza." Natural light from large expanses of window alters the colors of Lua during the day, bleaching it in spring, and mellowing it to a richer gold in fall and winter.

The color program at Lua turns sight into flavor— mango, papaya, turmeric, cayenne pepper—a spectrum of tropical, heated tones.

OPPOSITE **Necco-wafer colors of the bar tables cool the intense, sharp citrus and chili pepper tonalities used in the restaurant.**

BELOW **Banquette alcove seating is drenched with light.**

OVERLEAF **Nightime views of Manhattan provide strong visual contrast with the heat and vibrant activity at Lua.**

Monosaturate

BENJAMIN NORIEGA-ORTIZ

Noriega-Ortiz uses color without restraint, identifying it as the very essence of his work. He wants his super-saturated rooms to be overwhelming, to elicit the maximum emotional response. These bedrooms, one a guest room and the other the master bedroom, are part of a spacious Manhattan loft. He considers the dark blue a deep, powdery French blue and the crimson a Pompeian red. The red is the owners' favorite color, and they had no issue with drenching their room for repose with such a vibrant hue.

Noriega-Ortiz's bold dynamic in using color of this strength is to virtually erase the very notion of furnishings. That decision worked for both bedrooms—the carpets and fabrics were givens, pieces that he worked around. The only custom addition in the blue guestroom is the chair upholstered in leather that was dyed to match the paint. The white feathered lampshade was designed by Noriega-Ortiz to pierce through the darkness and is described by him as custom couture lighting.

Full-height draperies in rich claret line a hallway off the master suite.

Noriega-Ortiz erased the differences between styles of furniture with a single shade of deep French blue. A white feathered lamp, white leather armchair, and white-topped table add punch.

The lime-bleached floor softens the intensity of a Pompeian red master suite. Mirror-paneled walls double the impact of the rich red.

Photography Credits

Daniel Aubry: 143, 144–145, 146, 147, 148, 149, 150–151

Philip Beaurline: 39, 40–41, 42–43, 44, 45, 46, 47, 48–49

Antoine Bootz: 105, 106–107, 108, 109, 110, 111, 112, 113, 114–115, 116–117

Pieter Estersohn: 85, 86–87, 88, 89, 90, 91, 92–93, 94, 95

Tria Giovan: 97, 98, 99, 100–101, 102–103

Thibeault Jeansen: 135, 136, 137, 138, 139, 140–141

Nick Johnson: 165, 166–167, 168, 169, 170–171, 172–173

Michael Moran: 193, 194, 195, 196–197

Peter Murdock: 199, 200–201, 202–203

Inga Powilleit: 175, 176–177, 178, 179, 180, 181, 182, 183, 184–185, 186–187

Durston Saylor: 23, 24–25, 26, 27, 28, 29, 30–31

Robert Shimer/Hedrich Blessing: 33, 34, 35, 36, 37

Tim Street-Porter: 51, 52–53, 54–55, 56, 57, 58–59, 60–61, 73, 74–75, 76, 77, 78, 79, 80–81, 82–83

Kris Tamburello: 63, 64–65, 66–67, 68, 69, 70–71

Estate of John Vaughan: 189, 190, 191

Paul Warchol: 13, 14–15, 16, 17, 18, 19, 20–21

Claude Weber: 153, 154–155, 156, 157, 158, 159, 160, 161, 162, 163

Vicente Wolf: 119, 120, 121, 122–123

Patrick Wong: 125, 126–127, 128–129, 130, 131, 132, 133